THE AVIARY:
HOLIDAY
COCKTAILS

ALLEN & SARAH
HEMBERGER

MICAH MELTON

NICK KOKONAS

GRANT ACHATZ

INTRODUCTION

→ by Nick Kokonas

"How many of these drinks can I actually make?!"

That's a question that we've heard every day since we published *The Aviary Cocktail Book*. Our answer was always also a question: "How ambitious are you?" It's a bit coy. We do understand that much of the time you want a drink, not a project. But our intent with the Aviary book was to fully document our efforts over the course of a decade.

What you hold in your hands is very different. Our answer to your question is now: every drink in this cocktail manual, for every party, event, dinner, or game day that you host between Thanksgiving and the Super Bowl. These cocktails, punches, and ephemeral drinks are custom created to be accessible, delicious, *and* a bit ambitious. After all, you want a bit of 'wow' in your life – and a chance to impress your guests and your palate.

We've put together these recipes by adapting drinks and ideas we've presented at The Aviary exactly...but added the limitation that they must be makeable at home. Here are 28 totally unique fall and winter drinks that mix perfectly with the holidays and the food that typically accompanies your celebrations.

Here's an idea: rather than make the drinks yourself, get the ingredients and shakers together and set up a few stations around your home along with instructions on how to mix the cocktails. Each room becomes a new experiment. Your guests can mix it themselves...an interactive experience while they learn a few new skills – while saving you the trouble of shaking, stirring, and serving 80 cocktails over the course of an evening. I did this for a party at my own home and it was wildly fun and successful – while allowing me to actually enjoy myself as well.

However you decide to use *The Aviary: Holiday Cocktails*, make it your own. These drinks are meant to be modified and adapted to your own traditions. Have fun, experiment, and make mistakes.

And most of all, enjoy having friends and family close by...and an Aviary cocktail in hand.

Cheers!
Nick

BEFORE WE BEGIN

While *The Aviary Cocktail Book* seeks to faithfully present how we design recipes for use in our kitchens at The Aviary, the recipes we share in this booklet have been specifically crafted to be easy and fun to make at home. The following is some fundamental information to help get you started.

BASIC EQUIPMENT

The recipes in this booklet make use of a combination of kitchen and bar tools. These include:

Blender
We use durable, high-powered Vitamix blenders in our kitchens at The Aviary, but any reasonably well-made blender will work fine for these recipes.

Cocktail Mixing Glass
Also sometimes referred to as a cocktail stirring glass or tin, these containers are used to stir portions of cocktails with ice to chill them. Easy substitutes for these include a pint glass, a measuring cup, or a small mixing bowl (basically anything that can contain ice and some liquid).

Cocktail Shaker Tin
The aeration and small ice shards that result from shaking a cocktail with ice add textural interest to the beverage. The tool we use for this in our bar is a Koriko brand weighted stainless steel shaking tin – it is both durable and easy to clean. At home, a mason jar with a lid is an easy substitute.

Digital Scale
Digital scales are inexpensive and precise; we use them to measure almost every ingredient in our kitchens. When shopping for one of these tools, look for a scale that supports measurements accurate to ½ of a gram.

Digital Thermometer
Digital thermometers are easy to use, and are drastically faster and more accurate than analog thermometers.

Glass Bottles
We use various sizes of glass bottles to store juices, syrups, and many other cocktail components. In addition to being durable and nonreactive, glass bottles are also a familiar and comfortable form factor to work with for most bartenders. Mason jars or airtight plastic containers can also be used for storage of most recipes in this booklet.

Ice Molds
We have a slight obsession with collecting and using ice molds to create a wide variety of frozen shapes for our flavored ice, and we invite you to be adventurous when exploring this yourself. A common mold used in this booklet is a 1¼ inch silicone cube mold, easily found online.

Jigger
The standard tool for measuring ingredients for individual portions of cocktails, we use stainless steel, Japanese-style conical jiggers with indicator markings included on the inside surface. Small measuring cups with markings accurate to ¼oz can be used just as easily, or – in a pinch – measuring spoons (1 tbsp = ½oz).

Juicer
Many recipes call for the use of fresh citrus juices (please don't use pre-bottled "lemon" or "lime" juice from a plastic bottle shaped like the fruit). These can be produced with the use of a hand-held citrus press, a citrus reamer, or (in a pinch) a good forceful squeeze. Don't forget to strain the resulting juice through a mesh strainer to remove pulp or seeds.

Mixer
A countertop stand mixer – such as those made by Breville or KitchenAid – generally comes with multiple attachments that can be used for an assortment of tasks from softening butter to aerating cream. In a pinch, a whisk and some good old-fashioned elbow grease can suffice for most recipes in this booklet.

PEELERS/GRATERS

Y-Shaped Peelers - we use these inexpensive peelers to remove large citrus peels for garnish or expression.

Microplane - available in a variety of coarsenesses, these inexpensive and highly effective tools can be used for grating just about anything, from delicate fine citrus zest to hard spices.

STRAINING TOOLS

When we need to strain solids from a liquid, we do so using one of the following tools:

A fine mesh strainer, which consists of a conical or domed metal mesh and which usually has a handle.

A cocktail strainer, often referred to as a "Hawthorne strainer", which has a spring mechanism that can be used to adjust how finely or coarsely to strain small ice shards when pouring shaken drinks from cocktail tins.

Coffee filters are useful for removing the finest particles – as well as droplets of oil – from liquids. When straining a liquid through a coffee filter, be prepared to have some patience, as the process can take a while.

UNITS & MEASUREMENT

The units of measure we specify for length, weight, and temperature have been prioritized by the tools we use for the tasks we're performing. We almost exclusively use grams for weight, but you'll often see both weight and volume measurements used when portioning individual cocktails. This is because the jigger is typically the most comfortable and efficient measuring tool of the bartender during service, but some cocktails (such as those which are slushy or carbonated) are difficult to be reliably measured with this tool. Temperatures are expressed in both Fahrenheit and Celsius as a convenience, though the dominant preference is again set by the tool or device we're using (e.g. lab equipment like thermocirculators tend to prefer Celsius, while our oven dials are expressed in degrees Fahrenheit). These apparent inconsistencies are the result of using technologies from the bar world, the restaurant world, and the laboratory world in the same space at once.

BATCHING

At The Aviary, we pre-make many components of our cocktails before service, a process we refer to as "batching". Doing this allows us to focus our time on preparing everything we need before we open our doors for the day, so that we can serve drinks quickly and efficiently once guests arrive.

Home cooks face a similar situation when hosting holiday gatherings: much of the cooking is done in the time leading up to the party so that guests aren't waiting around for long periods of time before dining (imagine waiting for everyone to show up and only then putting the turkey in the oven!). To help with this, we've structured our recipes to be similar to how we handle them here in our kitchens, dividing things into individual components that can be prepared ahead of time and quickly assembled as needed for guests.

The shelf life of a batched component is highly dependent on its constituent ingredients: a batch comprising mostly bottled spirits can be made a day or more before it's consumed, whereas something using fresh juices can oxidize and lose its luster within an hour or two (citrus juices are a common and extreme example of the latter). A good general rule of thumb: if you notice citrus juices in a batched component, that component is best used the same day it's made.

A NOTE ON SUBSTITUTIONS

When considering the cost of gathering ingredients for cocktails, it can be tempting to consider substituting some of the spirits for what you may already have on-hand. Substitutions are a completely understandable prerogative in anyone's kitchen, and some may be done more seamlessly than others. We warmly invite experimentation and deviation from what we present here, while offering the necessary caveat that the resulting cocktail's flavor profile will be impacted accordingly. Be sure to taste and adjust your final creation and rebalance as necessary.

MISCELLANY

Here are a few definitions and explanations of terms, techniques, and conventions that are used throughout this booklet.

- Unless specified otherwise, all herbs and citrus juices should be fresh.
- To **split and scrape** a vanilla bean, halve it lengthwise with a sharp knife, then use the back edge of the knife to scrape the tiny seeds from the pod. Unless otherwise noted, use both the seeds and the pod in the recipe.
- To **double strain** a cocktail is to pour it from a cocktail shaker through both a Hawthorne strainer and a fine-mesh strainer in a single step. Generally the shaker tin and Hawthorne strainer are held in one hand, while the fine mesh strainer is held above the cocktail glass in the other hand. Double-straining removes ice shards from the cocktail.
- To **dry shake** a cocktail is to shake it vigorously in a cocktail shaker without ice. This technique is typically meant to aerate a drink before adding ice, which encourages a more frothy final result.

TABLE *of* CONTENTS

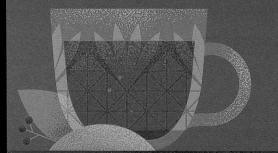
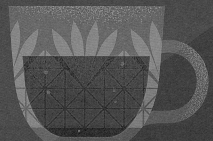

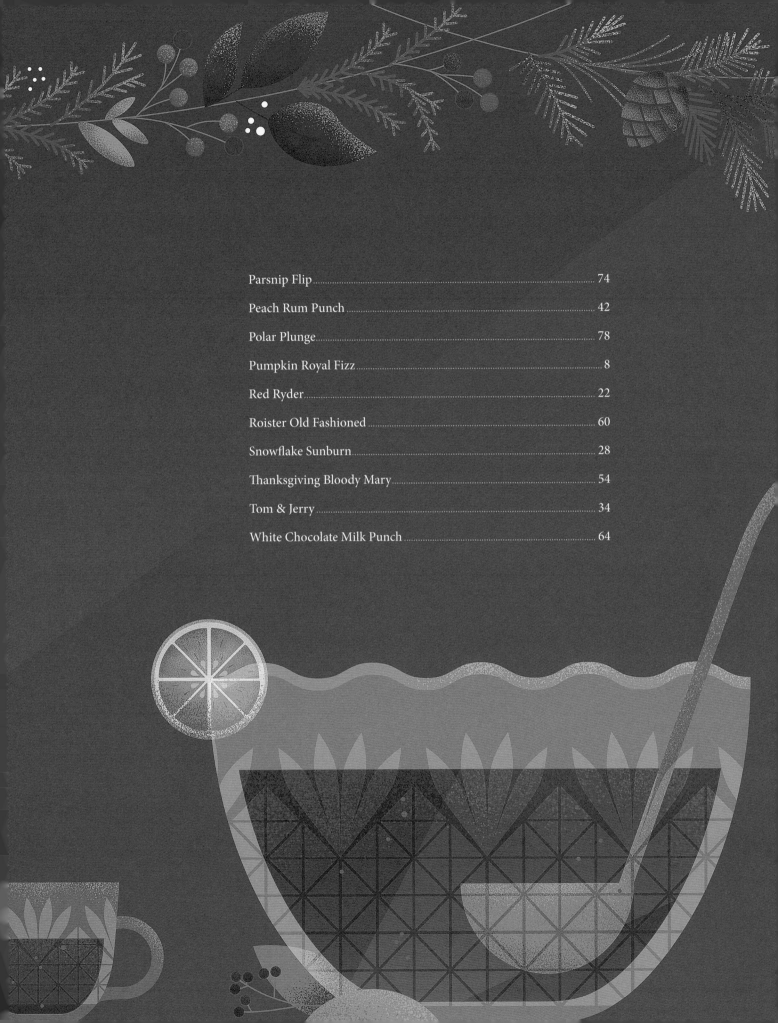

PUMPKIN ROYAL FIZZ

PUMPKIN STOCK BASE *(Serves 6)*

208g canned pumpkin purée
146g maple syrup
122g Uncle Nearest 1856 Whiskey
76g Clément Créole Shrubb
47g Ancho Reyes Ancho Chile Liqueur
11g Angostura Aromatic Bitters
7g pumpkin pie spice
2g kosher salt

Combine all ingredients in a blender. Blend on high speed for 1 minute to thoroughly mix. Strain the mixture with a mesh strainer into a clean bowl. Transfer to a glass bottle or other non-reactive airtight container and reserve in the refrigerator.

TO ASSEMBLE AND SERVE

3¼oz (97.5ml) pumpkin stock base
½oz (15ml) heavy cream
1 whole egg
3oz (90ml) sparkling water
1 cinnamon stick
1 whole nutmeg

Fill a tall serving glass halfway with ice. Combine pumpkin stock base, cream, and egg in a cocktail shaker. Dry shake until frothy. Add ice and shake again vigorously until chilled and diluted. Gently add the sparkling water into the serving glass, then double-strain the shaken cocktail mixture into the glass. Garnish with a generous grating of cinnamon and fresh nutmeg.

←
It's ok to use ground cinnamon or nutmeg here if you have trouble finding whole spices.

JUNIPER

GINGER SYRUP

200g fresh ginger, peeled and chopped against the fibers
200g sugar
100g hot water

Combine all ingredients in a blender, and blend at high speed for 1 minute. Strain the mixture through a mesh strainer to remove ginger fibers. Transfer the syrup to a glass bottle or other non-reactive airtight container and reserve in the refrigerator.

← This recipe yields more than is called for in the cocktail itself, but lesser amounts tend to be too small to be blended properly.

QUINCE STOCK

380g white grape juice
80g water
65g quince paste

Combine all ingredients in a medium saucepan, and bring the mixture to a simmer over medium heat. Transfer the mixture to a blender and blend at high speed for 1 minute. Allow the mixture to cool completely to room temperature. Reserve in the refrigerator.

← This mixture can settle out and separate over time; this is completely normal. Give it a good shake before using to re-incorporate everything.

SINGLE PORTION

JUNIPER

2oz (60ml) quince stock

1oz (30ml) St. George Terroir Gin

1oz (30ml) St. George Apple Brandy

¾oz (22.5ml) lime juice

¼oz (7.5ml) ginger syrup

1 candle

1 small juniper branch trimming

Combine all cocktail ingredients in a cocktail shaker, but don't add ice yet.

Light the candle. Using a pair of gardening or kitchen shears, trim a small sprig of juniper from a tip of the juniper branch. Hold one of the trimmed juniper sprigs just above the candle's flame until it begins smoking (try not to ignite the branch; you want it to smolder, which produces more fragrant smoke). Hold a medium serving glass upside-down over the juniper smoke to capture it.

Set the smoked glass onto your work surface, and add ice to the cocktail shaker. Shake briefly until chilled and diluted, then double-strain into the smoked glass.

BATCH

JUNIPER *(Serves 6)*

380g quince stock

165g St. George Terroir Gin

158g St. George Apple Brandy

141g lime juice

54g ginger syrup

Combine all ingredients in medium bowl, stirring to mix thoroughly. Strain into glass bottle. Transfer to refrigerator to chill thoroughly.

TO ASSEMBLE AND SERVE BATCH

1 candle

1 small juniper branch trimming

Light a candle. Using a pair of gardening or kitchen shears, trim 6 small sprigs of juniper from the tips of the juniper branch. Set these aside.

To serve cocktail, add 5oz (150ml) of the chilled cocktail base to a cocktail shaker, but don't add ice yet.

Hold one of the trimmed juniper sprigs just above the candle's flame until it begins smoking (try not to ignite the branch; you want it to smolder, which produces more fragrant smoke). Hold a medium serving glass upside-down over the juniper smoke to capture it.

Set the smoked glass onto your work surface, and add ice to the cocktail shaker. Shake briefly until chilled and diluted, then double-strain into the smoked glass.

Repeat for the remaining 5 cocktail portions, using a new juniper sprig for each glass.

CRAZY RICH RAISINS

GINGER SNAP SYRUP

300g water
300g sugar
10g ginger powder
200g ginger snap cookies

Combine water, sugar, and ginger powder in a small saucepan. Bring to a simmer over medium heat, whisking to dissolve sugar. Remove from heat and add the ginger snap cookies. Cover and allow to steep for 30 minutes. Gently pour the mixture through a fine mesh strainer, trying to leave as much of the cookie solids in the pot. Discard the strainer contents. Transfer the syrup to a small bottle or other non-reactive airtight container. Transfer to the refrigerator overnight to allow any remaining cookie sediment to settle to the bottom of the container. The next day, gently pour the syrup into a clean container, leaving any settled cookie sediment behind. Reserve in the refrigerator.

← Take care not to stir or break up the cookies once you've added them; doing so makes them difficult to strain out later, which ultimately leads to an undesirable cloudy sediment in the cocktail.

CRAZY RICH RAISINS BATCH
(Serves 6)

258g Diplomatico Rum Reserva Exclusiva
465g water
213g ginger snap syrup
90g Averna Amaro
60g Lustau Pedro Ximénez San Emilio Sherry
50g fresh lemon juice
30g ginger, peeled and sliced thinly against the fibers
25g golden raisins
20g orange peel, removed with a vegetable peeler
12g Angostura Aromatic Bitters
1g kosher salt
2 dried dates, halved, pits removed

Combine all ingredients in a medium saucepan. Bring to a simmer over medium heat. Remove from heat, cover, and let steep for 10 minutes. Strain the mixture through a mesh strainer, discarding solids.

At this point, the mixture is ready to serve while it is still warm. If you'd like to serve it later, allow it to cool to room temperature, then transfer to a glass bottle or other non-reactive airtight container, and reserve it in the refrigerator. The mixture can then be rewarmed in a small covered saucepan before portioning and serving.

TO PORTION AND SERVE BATCH

Gather 6 coffee mugs or tea cups, and warm them in a microwave for about 45 seconds (or, alternatively, warm them in an oven set to its lowest setting).

Transfer 5oz (150ml) of the cocktail mixture to a warmed mug and serve. Repeat for remaining mugs.

FATHER
KNOWS
BEST

The inspiration for this drink comes from just wanting to feel super-cozy on a cold evening, sitting next to a fireplace, snuggled under a nice thick blanket.

ROOT BEER SYRUP

270g Dad's Root Beer, room temperature
130g sugar

Combine the root beer and sugar in a medium bowl, whisking to dissolve sugar completely. Transfer to a glass bottle or other airtight container and reserve in the refrigerator.

FATHER KNOWS BEST

1½oz (45ml) The Macallan 12-year scotch whisky
½oz (15ml) Jägermeister
¼oz (7.5ml) Green Chartreuse
¼oz (7.5ml) root beer syrup
1 candle
small wood chips

Combine all cocktail ingredients in a cocktail mixing glass, but don't add ice yet.

Light the candle. Grasping a wood chip with small tongs or tweezers, hold it just above the candle's flame until it begins smoking (if it ignites, gently blow it out so that it smolders). Hold a medium serving glass upside-down over the smoke to capture it.

Set the smoked glass onto your work surface, and add ice to the cocktail mixing glass. Stir until chilled and diluted, then strain into the smoked glass.

Note: Suitable wood chips for this are those often sold for use in small smoker boxes for bbq grills; avoid wood that's been treated with paint or sealants. We prefer applewood chips, though other fruit or hard woods work just as well.

FATHER KNOWS BEST *(Serves 6)*

250g The Macallan 12-year scotch whisky
84g Jägermeister
42g Green Chartreuse
54g root beer syrup
180g water

Combine all ingredients in mixing bowl, stirring to combine thoroughly. Transfer to a non-reactive airtight container or a glass bottle. Reserve in freezer to chill thoroughly.

TO ASSEMBLE AND SERVE BATCH

1 candle
small wood chips

Light the candle. Grasping a wood chip with small tongs or tweezers, hold it just above the candle's flame until it begins smoking (if it ignites, gently blow it out so that it smolders). Hold a medium serving glass upside-down over the smoke to capture it.

Set the smoked glass onto your work surface, and add 3.5oz (105ml) of the chilled cocktail base.

Repeat for the remaining 5 cocktail portions, using a new wood chip for each glass.

CIDER MARGARITA

SIMPLE SYRUP

100g sugar
100g hot water

Combine the sugar and water in a medium bowl. Stir with a spatula to completely dissolve the sugar. Transfer to a glass bottle or other airtight container and reserve in the refrigerator.

SPICED CIDER

10g cinnamon sticks, crushed/broken into small pieces
6 whole star anise pods
500g apple cider
½ vanilla bean, split lengthwise (or 5g vanilla extract)
½g (about 1 tsp) freshly-grated nutmeg
6g fresh lemon peel, removed with a peeler

Fill a large bowl with ice, and set a smaller bowl inside it. In a medium saucepan, toast the cinnamon and star anise over medium heat. When the spices have darkened slightly and are very fragrant, carefully add the cider, vanilla, and nutmeg and bring to a boil. Remove the pot from the heat, add the lemon peel, cover, and allow to steep for 20 minutes. Strain the mixture through a mesh strainer into the bowl set in ice and allow it to cool completely. Transfer to a glass bottle or other non-reactive airtight container and reserve in the refrigerator.

CRANBERRY ICE

672g cranberry juice cocktail
68g sugar
10g fresh rosemary leaves
112g lemon juice
46g Tequila Fortaleza Reposado

Combine the cranberry and sugar in a medium saucepan and bring to a boil over medium heat, whisking to dissolve sugar. Remove from heat, add the rosemary, cover, and allow to steep for 10 minutes. Strain the mixture using a mesh strainer, discarding solids. Add the lemon juice and the tequila, stirring to combine. Fill a 1¼ inch (3.2 cm) square ice mold with mixture. Freeze into cubes until completely solid. Reserve.

←

We wrap unused partial vanilla beans in plastic wrap – squeezing out excess air to prevent them from drying out – and store them in an airtight container in a cool, dark place (but not in the refrigerator, which can promote excess moisture that encourages molding). Vanilla stored in this way can have a shelf life of about 6 months.

←

Pure cranberry juice lacks much sugar and is quite acidic; this recipe has been balanced using a sweetened cranberry juice product, often labeled as "cranberry cocktail".

SINGLE PORTION

CIDER MARGARITA

1½oz (45ml) Tequila Fortaleza Reposado

1oz (30ml) spiced cider

¾oz (22.5ml) fresh lemon juice

½oz (15ml) simple syrup

½ vanilla bean *(optional)*

Place 2 cubes of cranberry ice into a medium serving glass. Combine all ingredients (except the vanilla bean) with ice in a cocktail shaker. Shake vigorously until chilled and diluted, then strain through a fine mesh strainer into glass over ice. Cut a slit in one end of the vanilla bean half, opening it slightly to allow it to infuse as it sits in the drink. Insert the vanilla bean into the glass.

BATCH

CIDER MARGARITA *(Serves 6)*

240g Tequila Fortaleza Reposado

192g spiced cider

120g fresh lemon juice

96g simple syrup

Combine all ingredients in a medium bowl, stirring to mix thoroughly. Transfer the mixture to a glass bottle, and reserve at room temperature before serving.

TO ASSEMBLE AND SERVE BATCH

½ vanilla bean *(optional)*

Place 2 cubes of cranberry ice into a medium serving glass. Combine 4.25oz (127.5ml) of the cocktail base with ice in a cocktail shaker. Shake vigorously until chilled and diluted, then strain through a fine mesh strainer into glass over ice. Cut a slit in one end of the vanilla bean half, opening it slightly to allow it to infuse as it sits in the drink. Insert the vanilla bean into the glass.

RED RYDER

MADEIRA SYRUP

225 g Blandy's Rainwater Madeira
150 g sugar

Bring the madeira to a simmer in a small saucepan, and simmer until it's reduced to 100 g (or by about half its volume). Remove from the heat and add the sugar, stirring to dissolve. Cover and allow the syrup to cool completely, then transfer it to a glass bottle or other non-reactive airtight container and reserve in the refrigerator.

Note: the next steps involve flaming alcohol, which is obviously dangerous and can cause glassware to shatter if left to linger too long. It's best, therefore, to move through the assembly of this cocktail carefully but expeditiously.

Warming the serving vessel(s) in a microwave or an oven set to its lowest setting will help the mixture ignite more easily, and will also keep the cocktail warm for longer.

SINGLE PORTION

RED RYDER

1oz (30ml) Blandy's Rainwater Madeira

1oz (30ml) water

½oz (15ml) Jagermeister

½oz (15ml) Suntory Whisky Toki

⅛oz (3.75ml) crème de violette

1oz (30ml) Sacred Bond Brandy

½oz (15ml) madeira syrup

1 lemon peel

Combine the madeira, water, Jagermeister, whisky, and violet liqueur in a medium heat-proof measuring cup. Place the cup in a microwave and heat it for about 30 seconds, or until very warm but not boiling (you can also heat this in a small saucepan on an oven top if you do not have access to a microwave.)

Meanwhile, combine the brandy and madeira syrup in a serving mug. Using a stick lighter, carefully ignite this mixture. Express the lemon peel over the glass. Discard the peel.

Carefully add the heated cocktail portion from above. Allow any flames to extinguish naturally before drinking.

BATCH

RED RYDER BASE *(Serves 6)*

192g Blandy's Rainwater Madeira

180g water

78g Jagermeister

78g Suntory Whisky Toki

21g crème de violette

Combine all ingredients in a medium bowl, stirring to mix thoroughly. Transfer to a glass bottle or other non-reactive airtight container. Reserve at room temperature.

TO PORTION AND SERVE BATCH

1oz (30ml) Sacred Bond Brandy

½oz (15ml) madeira syrup

1 lemon peel

Transfer the batched cocktail base to a small saucepan, and place over medium heat. Bring the mixture to just under a simmer. Remove from heat.

Combine the brandy and madeira syrup in a serving mug. Using a stick lighter, carefully ignite this mixture. Express the lemon peel over the glass. Discard the peel. Carefully add 100g of the heated cocktail portion to the mug. Allow any flames to extinguish naturally before drinking. Repeat for remaining cocktail portions.

EXPRESSING
CITRUS PEELS

Squeezing a citrus peel (often referred to as "expressing" in the bar world) over a drink releases a spray of highly-aromatic oil, which floats on the surface of the drink. This provides a bright perfume that's generally meant to complement the flavors of the cocktail.

To express a peel, grasp it between your thumb and forefinger, with the exterior of the peel facing away from your hand. Holding the peel close to the cocktail, pinch it firmly, which will cause a fine mist of oil to spray from the peel onto the beverage. The peel can then be either discarded or used as a garnish.

SNOWFLAKE SUNBURN

WALNUT CINNAMON ORGEAT

50g walnuts

11.5g cinnamon sticks, crushed/broken into small pieces

300g warm water

190g sugar

1 small pinch cayenne powder

Preheat your oven to 350°F (175°C). Spread the walnuts on a cookie sheet and toast them in oven for about 15 minutes, or until they're deep brown and fragrant. Remove the sheet from the oven and let the walnuts cool completely.

In a medium saucepan, toast the cinnamon pieces over medium heat. When the cinnamon has darkened slightly and is very fragrant, carefully add the warm water, toasted walnuts, and then all remaining ingredients. Bring this mixture to a simmer. Adjust heat to low, cover, and cook for 20 minutes. Remove the mixture from the heat and allow to cool to room temperature (this can take around 2 hours). Transfer the mixture to a food processor or a blender, and pulse it once or twice, just to break things up a bit (you still want some larger pieces of cinnamon and walnut, so don't go too crazy here). Pour the mixture into an airtight container, cover, and transfer to the refrigerator for 8 to 24 hours to allow flavors to infuse.

Strain the mixture using a mesh strainer, discarding solids. Transfer to a glass bottle or other non-reactive airtight container. Reserve in the refrigerator.

← The touch of cayenne here helps boost the perceived "spiciness" of the cinnamon.

SNOWFLAKE SUNBURN
Single Portion

1½oz (45ml) Pierre Ferrand 1840 Cognac

1oz (30ml) walnut cinnamon orgeat

¾oz (22.5ml) fresh lemon juice

¾oz (22.5ml) St. George Pear Brandy

½oz (15ml) Cointreau

1 fresh mint sprig

Place a few cubes of ice into a medium serving glass. Combine all ingredients (except the mint) with ice in a cocktail shaker. Shake until chilled and diluted, then double-strain into the serving glass. Garnish with the mint sprig and a small straw.

SNOWFLAKE SUNBURN
Batch (Serves 6)

268g Pierre Ferrand 1840 Cognac

213g walnut cinnamon orgeat

144g fresh lemon juice

129g St. George Pear Brandy

98g Cointreau

Combine all ingredients in a medium bowl, stirring to mix thoroughly. Transfer mixture to a glass bottle or other non-reactive airtight container. Reserve in the refrigerator.

To serve, combine 4¼oz (127.5ml) of this cocktail base with ice in a cocktail shaker. Shake until chilled and diluted, then double-strain into a serving glass containing a few cubes of ice. Garnish with a fresh mint sprig and a small straw.

KEEPING MINT FRESH

If you intend to serve cocktails with a mint garnish at a holiday gathering, you may run into a problem we routinely encounter at The Aviary: keeping sprigs of mint fresh and bright over the course of your "service". The following method, first popularized by barman Peter Vestinos, will keep mint fresh and ready for use for around 8–10 hours (the length of a typical bar service).

1

Most fresh mint found in supermarkets comes packaged in small plastic containers; the mint is often cramped and wilted, and while it may taste fine, it can be a bit visually unappealing.

2

To freshen the mint, first fill a large bowl with ice and cold water.

Gather your fresh mint, and trim off any leaves below the topmost "crown" of each sprig. Reserve these spare leaves for another use.

Using a sharp knife, cut away the lower ends of the mint sprigs on a bias (similar to how you'd trim the stems of fresh flowers).

3

4

Plunge the trimmed mint springs – head first – into the ice bath. This step firms and brightens the mint leaves, leaving them looking full and plump.

5

Fill a coffee mug or other small cup two-thirds with warm (not hot) water. Transfer the mint sprigs to this cup, and place the cup near your work area from where you will be serving cocktails.

CARAMEL
APPLE SOUR

HIBISCUS ICE

285 g water

83 g sugar

10 g dried hibiscus flowers or hibiscus tea

1 small pinch salt

86 g POM pomegranate juice

45 g Croft Ruby Port

35 g lemon juice

1 g rosewater

Combine the water, sugar, hibiscus, and salt in a medium saucepan and bring to a boil over medium heat, whisking to dissolve sugar. Remove from heat, cover, and allow to steep for 1 hour. Strain the mixture using a mesh strainer, discarding solids. Add the remaining ingredients, stirring to combine. Fill a 1¼ inch (3.2 cm) square ice mold with mixture. Freeze into cubes until completely solid. Reserve.

POMEGRANATE CARAMEL

250 g dark brown sugar

7 g cinnamon sticks

5 whole cloves

2 whole star anise pods

½ vanilla bean, split and scraped

1 g salt

360 g POM pomegranate juice

200 g sweetened condensed milk

In a medium saucepan, combine the brown sugar, cinnamon, cloves, star anise, vanilla seeds and pod, salt, and 60 g of the pomegranate juice. Bring this mixture to a boil over medium-high heat, and boil for 6 minutes, stirring constantly to keep any of the ingredients from scorching. Remove the pot from the heat, and slowly add the remaining pomegranate juice (be careful; the melted sugar mixture is very hot and will splatter at first), stirring to combine. Add the condensed milk and mix thoroughly. Strain the mixture through a fine mesh strainer, discarding solids. Transfer to an airtight container and reserve in the refrigerator.

TO ASSEMBLE AND SERVE

2 oz (60 ml) Rhine Hall Oak Aged Apple Brandy

1¼ oz (37.5 ml) pomegranate caramel

¾ oz (22.5 ml) fresh lemon juice

¾ oz (22.5 ml) egg white

1 lemon peel

Place 2 cubes of hibiscus ice into a medium serving glass. Combine all ingredients (except lemon peel) in a cocktail shaker. Dry shake until frothy. Add ice and shake again vigorously until chilled and diluted, then strain into the serving glass over ice. Express the lemon peel over the glass. Discard the peel.

TOM & JERRY

While at first glance this cocktail seems to resemble a typical holiday eggnog recipe, a classic Tom & Jerry is meant to be served warm rather than cold. Our version is built on a rich, vanilla-flavored *sabayon*, with a lovely complexity offered by the use of a few amari and a funky Jamaican-style rum.

TOM & JERRY BASE

70g Averna Amaro
66g Zaya Gran Reserva Rum
15g Smith & Cross Rum, optional
43g Licor 43 Original
2g Angostura Aromatic Bitters

Combine all ingredients in medium bowl, stirring to mix thoroughly. Cover and set aside.

TOM & JERRY BATCH *(Serves 8–10)*

1 vanilla bean
4 egg yolks
382g heavy cream
1 pinch freshly-grated nutmeg
500g whole milk
100g sugar
6g kosher salt

Fill a small pot with an inch or so of water, and bring it to a simmer over medium-high heat.

Meanwhile, cut the vanilla bean in half lengthwise with a sharp, small knife. Use the rear edge of the knife to scrape the tiny seeds from each pod half. Set the pod halves aside for a moment. Transfer the vanilla seeds to a small mixing bowl, and add the egg yolks, cream, and freshly-grated nutmeg, whisking to combine everything thoroughly.

Set the mixing bowl over the simmering pot of water, whisking the mixture slowly until it thickens a bit and is slightly steaming (be patient; this step could take a while). When the mixture gets to be the consistency of heavy whipping cream (which should happen at around 180°F), remove the bowl from the heat and set it aside.

Continued →

Tom and Jerry

TOM & JERRY BATCH *continued*

Combine the whole milk, sugar, salt, and the scraped vanilla pod halves in a medium saucepan. Warm the mixture over medium-high heat, whisking to dissolve the sugar and to keep things moving as it heats. Allow the mixture to come to a simmer, take care not to boil it outright (which could impart undesirable flavors from the scalded milk). Remove the saucepan from the heat, and use tongs or a strainer to remove the vanilla pod.

Slowly whisk the heated milk into the seasoned egg mixture, adding very small amounts of the heated milk at first. Once the heated milk and egg mixtures have been fully incorporated, whisk in the Tom & Jerry alcoholic base mixture.

At this point, the cocktail is ready and best served right away. If you need to hold it for a while, you can transfer it to a pre-warmed crock pot set on low heat, or into a bowl set over simmering water.

TO PORTION AND SERVE BATCH

1 nutmeg

Using a ladle, dole out servings into individual glasses, topping each with a small grating of fresh nutmeg.

←

This process – called "tempering" – ensures that you don't scramble the eggs in the egg mixture by heating it too quickly.

BEAM ME UP, TODDY

BROWN BUTTER

60g unsalted butter

Fill a medium bowl with ice water, and set a smaller bowl inside of it. Place the butter into a small saucepan, and set this over medium-high heat. Brown the butter – it will first melt, then froth. As the froth subsides and the butter takes on a nutty brown color and aroma, remove it from the heat. Pour it carefully into the bowl set over ice, trying to leave as much of the burnt butter solids behind in the pot as possible. Allow the butter to cool and solidify. Reserve it in a small covered container at room temperature.

BEAM ME UP, TODDY BASE BATCH
(Serves 8–10)

525g water

135g clover honey

130g Jim Beam Single Barrel Bourbon

100g Noilly Prat Dry Vermouth

80g St. George Pear Brandy

80g Grand Marnier

0.5g kosher salt

Combine all ingredients in medium saucepan, whisking to dissolve honey. Reserve covered at room temperature until ready to serve.

TO ASSEMBLE AND SERVE

2 lemons

2 oranges

2 bags (about 5g) Earl Grey tea

3 sprigs of sage

113g dried cranberries

77g yuzu juice

Peel the lemons and oranges using a vegetable peeler, taking care to remove as little pith as possible. Arrange the citrus peels, tea, sage, and cranberries in a large French press pot. Add the yuzu juice to the press pot.

Using a small spoon, place a small dollop (about 1 tsp) of brown butter into the bottom of a serving glass. Repeat for remaining serving glasses.

Bring the cocktail base to a boil. Remove mixture from heat and pour into French press. Allow to steep for 4 minutes. After this time, depress the plunger on the press, and pour about 3½oz (105ml) into each serving glass, stirring slightly to melt butter. Serve warm.

NON-ALCOHOLIC
BEAM ME UP, TODDY

BROWN BUTTER   60g unsalted butter

Fill a medium bowl with ice water, and set a smaller bowl inside of it. Place the butter into a small saucepan, and set this over medium-high heat. Brown the butter – it will first melt, then froth. As the froth subsides and the butter takes on a nutty brown color and aroma, remove it from the heat. Pour it carefully into the bowl set over ice, trying to leave as much of the burnt butter solids behind in the pot as possible. Allow the butter to cool and solidify. Reserve it in a small covered container at room temperature.

**NON-ALCOHOLIC
BEAM ME UP, TODDY
BASE**
Batch (Serves 6)

480g pear juice
180g freshly-squeezed orange juice
135g clover honey
215g water
0.5g kosher salt

Combine all ingredients in medium bowl, whisking to dissolve honey. Reserve covered at room temperature.

TO ASSEMBLE
AND SERVE
BATCH

2 lemons

2 oranges

4 bags (about 10g) Earl Grey tea

3 sprigs of sage

113g dried cranberries

55g yuzu juice

20g fresh lemon juice

Peel the lemons and oranges using a vegetable peeler, taking care to remove as little pith as possible. Arrange the citrus peels, tea, sage, and cranberries in a French press pot. Add the yuzu juice and lemon juice to the press pot.

Using a small spoon, place a small dollop (about 1 tsp) of brown butter into the bottom of a serving glass. Repeat for remaining 5 serving glasses.

In a medium saucepan, bring the cocktail base to a boil. Remove mixture from heat and pour into French press. Allow to steep for 4 minutes. After this time, depress the plunger on the press, and pour about 3½oz (105ml) into each serving glass, stirring slightly to melt butter. Serve warm.

PEACH
RUM
PUNCH

ICE BLOCK   Craft a large block of clear ice using the method detailed on the following pages (p 46–47), ensuring that the block neatly fits into your punch serving bowl. Reserve ice block in the freezer until ready to serve.

PEACH ELDERFLOWER ICE

5 lemons
2 oranges
80 g sugar
450 g peach nectar
100 g water
60 g St. Germain Elderflower Liqueur

Peel the lemons and oranges using a vegetable peeler, taking care to remove as little pith as possible. Reserve the peeled fruit for juicing. In a small bowl, combine the peels and sugar. Muddle this mixture with cocktail muddler or the end of a rolling pin. Allow to sit for 30 minutes, muddling and stirring periodically.

Meanwhile, juice the lemons and oranges separately, straining the juices through a fine mesh strainer to remove pulp and seeds.

In a medium bowl, combine 115 g fresh orange juice and 110 g fresh lemon juice with the peach nectar, water, and St. Germain, stirring to mix thoroughly (reserve any remaining lemon juice for the final cocktail assembly). Pour this mixture over the citrus peel mixture, stirring to dissolve the sugar. Strain this mixture through a fine mesh strainer, discarding solids.

Fill a 1¼ inch (3.2 cm) square ice mold with mixture. Freeze into cubes until completely solid. Reserve.

PUNCH BASE BATCH
(Serves 8–10)

2 lemons
130 g sugar
500 g water
4 bags (about 8 g) chai tea
216 g Caravedo Mosto Verde Pisco
208 g Plantation O.F.T.D. Rum
32 g Giffard Crème de Pêche

Peel the lemons using a vegetable peeler, taking care to remove as little pith as possible. Reserve the peeled fruit for juicing. In a small bowl, combine the lemon peels and sugar. Muddle this mixture with cocktail muddler or the end of a rolling pin. Allow to sit for 30 minutes, muddling and stirring periodically.

In small saucepan, bring the water to a simmer. Meanwhile, place the chai tea in the bowl with the lemon peel mixture. Set a timer for 4 minutes. Add 475 g of simmering water, stirring gently to dissolve the sugar and periodically dunking the tea bags to aid with flavor extraction. When the timer is up, strain the mixture through a mesh strainer, discarding solids.

← We simmer more water than we actually use to account for loss due to evaporation.

In a medium bowl, combine the lemon-chai mixture with the remaining ingredients, stirring to mix thoroughly. Transfer to a glass bottle or other non-reactive airtight container and transfer to the refrigerator to chill thoroughly.

TO ASSEMBLE AND SERVE

4-6 lemons, including those reserved from the above Punch Base recipe
nutmeg

Peel the lemons using a vegetable peeler, trying to remove peel in large swaths and taking care to remove as little pith as possible. Using a cookie cutter, cut small shapes from peels (or alternatively, trim into rectangles). Set these aside.

Juice the lemons, straining the juices through a fine mesh strainer to remove pulp and seeds.

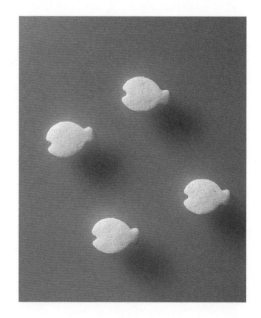

Place a large clear block of ice into a punch bowl or other large serving vessel. Pour the punch base over the ice. Add 115 g fresh lemon juice, stirring to combine and to dilute the mixture slightly.

To serve, place 2 peach elderflower ice cubes into a punch glass. Ladle punch from bowl into glass over ice. Garnish with 1 reserved lemon peel and a grating of fresh nutmeg.

CLEAR ICE

Crafting clear ice at home is relatively simple and easy. The following method – originally popularized by cocktails expert Camper English – requires only simple tools, a bit of freezer space, and some patience.

1

Fill an insulated container (such as a small travel cooler) with water, and transfer the container to your freezer. Ensure that the container remains uncovered (you can remove the lid of the container if need be).

2

The water will freeze from the top downwards, pushing down impurities as it goes. Allow the ice block to freeze at least halfway down (it's fine – but not necessary – to allow it to freeze completely); the upper part of the block should remain very clear. Remove the block from the container and allow it to warm a bit – this process is called "tempering" and is critical to cleanly-cutting the ice. When the block is tempered, its outer surface will transform from cloudy and frosted to slick and wet-looking.

Continue scoring and tapping the block to
separate it into smaller pieces or shaping it to
fit into your desired serving vessel.

4

Use a serrated bread knife to score the ice
block, then lightly tap the back of the knife
blade with a mallet. After a few taps, the ice
should crack cleanly along your score lines. Use
this method to cut off and remove any sections
of the block that are cloudy internally. If you
notice any jagged cracks or shards, stop and
allow the ice to temper further.

3

Once you've formed your desired shapes,
return your ice to the freezer to store until
ready to serve.

5

HAY *is for* HORSES

SIMPLE SYRUP

25g sugar

25g hot water

Combine sugar and water in medium bowl. Stir with spatula to completely dissolve sugar. Transfer to glass bottle and reserve in refrigerator.

HORSERADISH STOCK

400g hot water

100g prepared horseradish

Combine the water and horseradish in a medium bowl, whisking to combine. Allow the mixture to steep for 1 hour. Strain through a mesh strainer, discarding solids and reserving the liquid.

GRAPEFRUIT ICE

400g horseradish stock

200g fresh grapefruit juice

60g Giffard Crème de Pamplemousse Rose

40g simple syrup

20g Tanqueray 10 gin

Combine all ingredients in a medium bowl, whisking to mix thoroughly. Fill a 1¼ inch (3.2 cm) square ice mold with mixture. Freeze into cubes until completely solid. Reserve.

TANQUERHAY

400g Tanqueray 10 gin

60g fresh hay

Preheat oven to 350°F (205°C). Spread the hay onto a cookie sheet or sheet tray. Toast the hay in the oven for 1 hour. Remove from oven and allow to cool completely.

Transfer the hay and gin into a zip-top bag or other non-reactive airtight container, and allow to infuse for 1 day. After this time, strain the mixture through a mesh strainer, discarding solids. Transfer the hay-infused gin to a glass bottle or other non-reactive container and reserve.

←

If you have trouble finding hay, you can substitute rolled oats, or can omit it completely... the final drink will still be tasty.

SINGLE PORTION

HAY IS FOR HORSES

1½oz (45ml) tanquerhay

¾oz (22.5ml) fresh lemon juice

¾oz (22.5ml) maple syrup

1 bar spoon (½ tsp, 5ml) rice wine vinegar

1½oz (45ml) Schramsberg Brut Rosé

1 grapefruit peel

Place 3 cubes of grapefruit ice into a medium serving glass. Combine all ingredients (except sparkling wine and grapefruit peel) with ice in a cocktail shaker. Shake vigorously until chilled and diluted, then strain through a fine mesh strainer into the serving glass. Gently add the sparkling wine. Express the grapefruit peel over the glass. Discard the peel.

BATCH

HAY IS FOR HORSES BASE *(Serves 6)*

243g tanquerhay

138g fresh lemon juice

162g maple syrup

9g rice wine vinegar

Combine all ingredients in a medium bowl, stirring to mix thoroughly. Transfer the mixture to a glass bottle. Reserve at room temperature.

TO ASSEMBLE AND SERVE BATCH

1½oz (45ml) Schramsberg Brut Rosé per portion

1 grapefruit peel per portion

Place 3 cubes of grapefruit ice into a medium serving glass. Combine 3oz (90ml) of the cocktail base with ice in a cocktail shaker. Shake vigorously until chilled and diluted, then strain through a fine mesh strainer into the serving glass. Gently add 1½oz (45ml) sparkling wine. Express the grapefruit peel over the glass. Discard the peel.

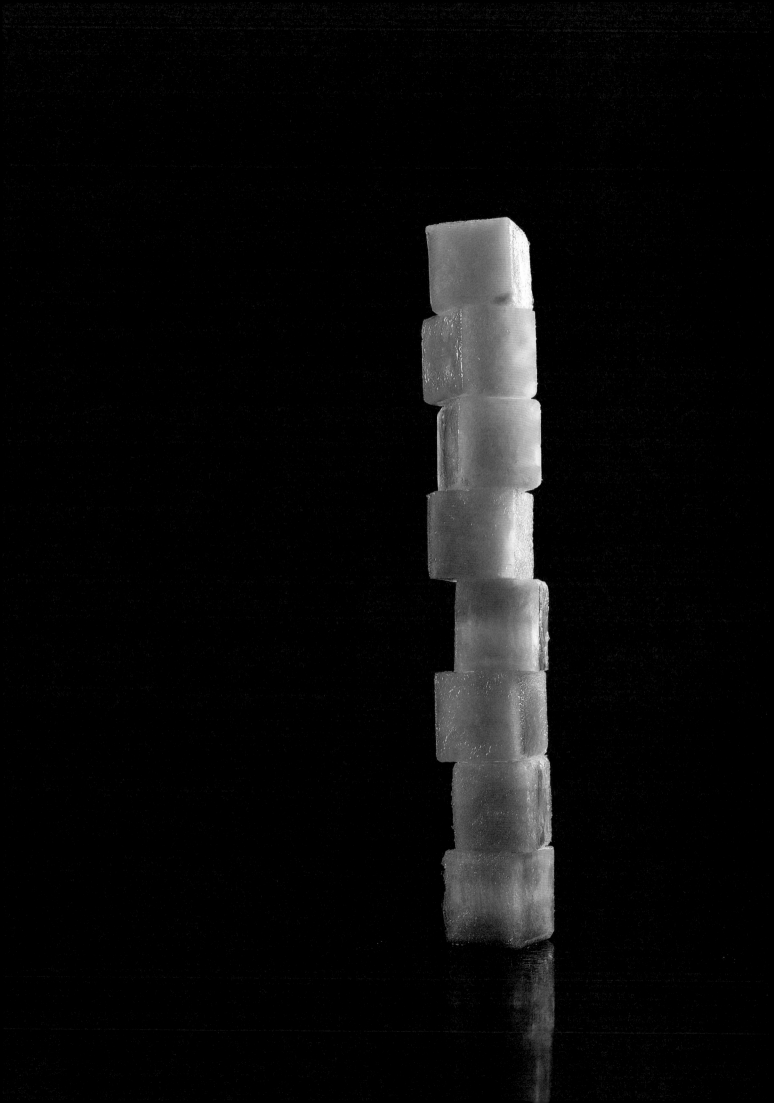

HAY *is for* HORSES

SIMPLE SYRUP

60g sugar
60g hot water

Combine the sugar and water in a medium bowl. Stir with a spatula to completely dissolve the sugar. Transfer to a glass bottle or other airtight container and reserve in the refrigerator.

HORSERADISH STOCK

400g hot water
100g prepared horseradish

Combine the water and horseradish in a medium bowl, whisking to combine. Allow the mixture to steep for 1 hour. Strain through a mesh strainer, discarding solids and reserving the liquid.

GRAPEFRUIT ICE

400g horseradish stock
200g fresh grapefruit juice
104g simple syrup
46g fresh lemon juice

Combine all ingredients in a medium bowl, whisking to mix thoroughly. Fill a 1¼ inch (3.2 cm) square ice mold with mixture. Freeze into cubes until completely solid. Reserve.

JUNIPER HAY STOCK

40g fresh hay
5g cinnamon sticks, crushed/broken into small pieces
5g coriander seeds
4 green cardamom pods, crushed
15g juniper berries
650g water
peel from ½ lime (about 5g)
peel from ½ orange (about 13g)

Preheat oven to 350°F (205°C). Spread the hay onto a cookie sheet or sheet tray. Toast the hay in the oven for 1 hour. Remove from oven and allow to cool completely.

Meanwhile, in a medium saucepan, toast the cinnamon, coriander, and cardamom over medium heat until fragrant. Let cool completely.

In a medium saucepan, combine the toasted hay, spices, and juniper with the water. Bring this to a simmer over medium heat. Remove from heat, add lime and orange peels, cover, and let steep for 1.5 hours. Strain this mixture through a mesh strainer, discarding solids. Transfer the liquid to a glass bottle or other non-reactive container and reserve.

←

If you have trouble finding hay, you can substitute rolled oats, or can omit it completely... the final drink will still be tasty.

←

This step pasteurizes the hay, and also brings out its fragrant aroma.

SINGLE PORTION

NON-ALCOHOLIC HAY IS FOR HORSES

2½oz (75ml) juniper hay stock

¾oz (22.5ml) fresh lemon juice

¾oz (22.5ml) maple syrup

1 bar spoon (½ tsp, 5ml) rice wine vinegar

1½oz (45ml) grapefruit-flavored sparkling water

1 grapefruit peel

Place 3 cubes of grapefruit ice into a medium serving glass. Combine all ingredients (except sparkling water and grapefruit peel) with ice in a cocktail shaker. Shake vigorously until chilled and diluted, then strain through a fine mesh strainer into glass over ice. Gently add the sparkling water. Express the grapefruit peel over the glass. Discard the peel.

BATCH

NON-ALCOHOLIC HAY IS FOR HORSES *(Serves 6)*

450g juniper hay stock

138g fresh lemon juice

162g maple syrup

9g rice wine vinegar

Combine all ingredients in a medium bowl, stirring to mix thoroughly. Transfer the mixture to a glass bottle. Reserve at room temperature.

To serve cocktail, place 3 cubes of grapefruit ice into a medium serving glass. Combine 3oz (90ml) of the chilled cocktail base with ice in a cocktail shaker. Shake vigorously until chilled and diluted, then strain through a fine mesh strainer into glass over ice. Gently add 1½oz (45ml) grapefruit-flavored sparkling water. Express the grapefruit peel over the glass. Discard the peel.

THANKSGIVING
BLOODY MARY

/

This recipe makes resourceful use of Thanksgiving leftovers,
leveraging the bones from a roasted turkey to build a flavorful
broth that serves as a base for this riff on a classic bloody mary.

/

TURKEY BROTH
(Optional)

Spread the bones and turkey scraps from a roasted turkey onto a cookie
sheet or sheet tray, and roast in an oven at 400°F (205°C) until very browned.
Transfer these to a large pot and cover with water. Bring to a boil, then lower
the heat to a slow simmer, cover, and cook for around 2 hours. Strain the
liquid, discarding solids. Chill the stock in an ice bath to cool it completely,
then transfer it to a large airtight container and reserve in the refrigerator.

**THANKSGIVING
BLOODY MARY BASE**
Batch (Serves 6)

794g (one 28oz can) whole peeled san marzano tomatoes

550g turkey broth

397g (one 14oz can) cranberry jelly

300g cranberries (fresh or frozen)

186g worcestershire sauce

40g fresh lemon juice

32g sambal

50g prepared horseradish

8g salt

8g celery salt

Combine all ingredients (except celery salt) in a large bowl, stirring to mix
thoroughly. Transfer mixture to a blender, working in batches if everything
won't fit at once. Blend at high speed for 1 minute to thoroughly incorporate
everything. Add celery salt and pulse blender briefly to combine. Strain through
a fine mesh strainer, discarding solids (you can skip this step if you prefer more
texture in your bloody mary). Transfer to a glass bottle or other non-reactive
airtight container and reserve in the refrigerator to chill thoroughly.

←

Store-bought chicken or turkey
broth can be substituted,
although we find the flavor
offered by a homemade stock
to be far better and worth the
extra effort.

←

More horseradish can
be used if you like
things extra spicy.

**TO ASSEMBLE
AND SERVE**

1oz (30ml) vodka

5oz (150ml) Thanksgiving bloody mary base

Fill a tall serving glass three-quarters full of ice. Pour vodka into glass, then add
cocktail base, stirring briefly to chill and incorporate. Repeat with remaining
cocktail portions. Serve.

←

You can omit the
vodka entirely if you'd
prefer to make this
cocktail non-alcoholic.

GLÖGG

Warm Mulled Wine

GLÖGG BATCH
(Serves 8–14)

2 oranges

10 allspice berries

12 green cardamom pods

12 whole cloves

2 star anise

3 cinnamon sticks

165 g Krogstad Aquavit

1500 ml (2 bottles) pinot noir

86 g ginger, peeled and sliced thinly against the fibers

140 g raisins

107 g slivered almonds

234 g sugar

283 g lingonberry preserves

0.5 g kosher salt

Peel the oranges using a vegetable peeler, taking care to remove as little pith as possible. Set the peel aside for a moment (the fruit itself is unused in this recipe, and can be reserved for another purpose).

Lightly crack the allspice and green cardamom with the bottom of a heavy dutch oven. Place these into the dutch oven, along with the cloves, star anise, and cinnamon sticks. Toast the spices over medium heat until fragrant. Remove the pot from the heat, slowly add Aquavit, then return the pot to the burner and bring the liquid to a boil. Add the reserved orange peel along with all remaining ingredients, and bring to a boil again. Remove from heat, cover, and allow the mixture to steep for 2 hours.

Strain the mixture through a fine mesh strainer, optionally discarding solids *(see note about garnishes below)*. Return the mixture to the dutch oven, cover, and reserve at room temperature until ready to serve.

TO PORTION AND SERVE BATCH

Return the dutch oven to the heat, and warm gently over medium heat. Optionally, transfer the mixture to a large heatproof punch bowl. Ladle into small serving glasses and serve.

Traditionally, this drink is garnished with a small spoonful of the raisins and almonds used to mull the wine (which would require a bit of careful separation of the strained solids from above). Alternative garnishes we like include a cinnamon stick, a star anise pod, a small piece of candied ginger, an orange wheel, or a fresh orange peel.

A middle-of-the-road pinot is a good choice here; something you would drink by itself, but nothing super fancy (because much of its nuance will be covered by other flavors).

←

←

Blackberry preserves can be substituted here if need be.

←

Pouring warm liquid from a large pot can be unwieldy at best, dangerous at worst. We often use a ladle to transfer warm liquids a bit at a time in cases like these.

ROISTER
OLD FASHIONED

/

To "roister" is to party boisterously. This cocktail, featured on
our eponymous restaurant's inaugural menu, riffs on a venerable
classic by adding some complexity thanks to the use of apple
brandy and a brown butter tincture.

/

DEMERARA
SYRUP

200g demerara sugar
100g water

In a small saucepan, stir together the sugar and water over medium heat just until the
sugar is completely dissolved. Remove from heat and let cool. Transfer the syrup to a
glass bottle and reserve in refrigerator.

BROWN BUTTER
TINCTURE

113g (1 stick) butter
113g high-proof neutral grain spirit (e.g. Everclear)

Place the butter into a small saucepan, and set this over medium-high heat. Brown
the butter – it will first melt, then froth. As the froth subsides and the butter takes
on a nutty brown color and aroma, remove it from the heat and all it to cool for a
few minutes.

If you don't have sous vide equipment:
Combine the melted brown butter and the neutral grain spirit in a non-reactive airtight
container (a mason jar works well for this). Store the jar in a warm location for 1 week,
shaking or stirring daily. After a week, place the jar in the freezer for 2 hours, or until
the butter has solidified. Strain the liquid through a fine mesh strainer, then through a
coffee filter. Transfer the strained liquid to a small glass container and reserve.

If you have an immersion circulator or sous vide bath:
Combine the melted brown butter and the neutral grain spirit in a vacuum bag
and seal. Cook en sous vide at 75°C (165°F) for 2 hours. Meanwhile, prepare an ice
bath. Transfer the bag to the ice bath to chill completely, then place the bag upright
in the freezer for 2 hours, or until the butter's fat solidifies. Using sharp scissors, cut a
small incision in the bottom corner of the bag and drain the liquid contents through
a coffee filter, leaving the solids behind. Transfer the strained liquid to a small glass
container and reserve.

SINGLE PORTION

ROISTER OLD FASHIONED

1¼oz (37.5ml) J. Rieger & Co. Kansas City Whiskey

1oz (30ml) Lustau Don Nuño Oloroso Sherry

¾oz (22.5ml) Laird's Jersey Lightning Apple Brandy

¼oz (7.5ml) demerara syrup

⅛oz (3.75ml) brown butter tincture

2 dashes Angostura Aromatic Bitters

1 navel orange peel, trimmed

Place a large chunk of ice into a medium serving glass. Combine all ingredients (except the orange peel) with ice in cocktail mixing glass. Stir until chilled and diluted. Strain mixture into the serving glass. Express the orange peel over the glass. Insert the peel into the glass alongside the ice chunk. Garnish the drink with 3 additional drops of brown butter tincture.

BATCH

ROISTER OLD FASHIONED (*Serves 6*)

233g J. Rieger & Co. Kansas City Whiskey

203g Lustau Don Nuño Oloroso Sherry

137g Laird's Jersey Lightning Apple Brandy

66g demerara syrup

21g brown butter tincture

13g Angostura Aromatic Bitters

190g water

Combine all ingredients in a medium bowl, stirring to mix thoroughly. Transfer the mixture to a glass bottle, and place in the freezer to chill thoroughly before serving.

TO PORTION AND SERVE BATCH

1 navel orange peel per portion

brown butter tincture

Place a large chunk of ice into a medium serving glass. Pour 4½oz (135ml) of the chilled cocktail base over the ice chunk in the glass. Express the orange peel over the glass. Insert the peel into the glass alongside the ice chunk. Garnish the drink with 3 additional drops of brown butter tincture.

Repeat with remaining 5 cocktail portions.

PRESENTING CITRUS PEELS

Trimming citrus peels is a straightforward and simple step that can dramatically enhance the visual presentation of cocktails. At The Aviary, we employ a handful of shapes and sizes, each chosen primarily for its relationship to the glassware we're using (we want a peel to look "properly-paired" with the glassware – extending its form, rather than looking too big or too small). It can be fun to get creative with this garnish, and there's no need to stop at just straight knife cuts; cookie cutters or other cutting tools can add interesting or playful forms that can suit the personality of your own bar.

When selecting oranges that may be used for their peels in addition to their fruit, be sure to look for those with bumpy, firm skin rather than a soft, shiny exterior. The former indicates peel that is plump and full of oil.

WHITE CHOCOLATE
MILK PUNCH

SALT SOLUTION

50 g water
17 g kosher salt

Combine water and salt in a medium bowl. Whisk mixture until no more salt will dissolve; some salt will remain in the bowl (this is an indication that the water is fully-saturated with salt, which is what we want). Strain the solution through a mesh strainer, discarding the excess salt. Transfer the solution to a small glass dropper bottle or other non-reactive airtight container. Reserve.

CINNAMON BOURBON

100 g J.T.S Brown 100 Proof Bottled In Bond Kentucky Bourbon
3 g cinnamon sticks

Combine the bourbon and cinnamon sticks in a small glass bottle or other non-reactive airtight container. Allow this mixture to infuse for 3 days. Reserve.

CARAMELIZED WHITE CHOCOLATE MILK

250 g white chocolate, coarsely chopped
500 g whole milk

If you don't have sous vide equipment:
Bring a large pot of water to a simmer. Seal the white chocolate in a heavy-duty zip-top bag, trying to remove as much air as possible before closing. Dip the bag into the simmering water, taking care to keep it off the bottom of the pot so the plastic doesn't burn (you can clip it to the side of the pot using a clothespin to help with this). Simmer the bag for about 5 hours, or until the chocolate has taken on a deep tan color.

If you have an immersion circulator or sous vide bath:
Seal the white chocolate in a vacuum bag. Cook en sous vide at 95°C (200°F) for 5 hours.

When the chocolate is nearly done, bring the milk to a simmer over medium heat, taking care not to let it scald. Remove the milk from the heat. Transfer the caramelized white chocolate to a medium bowl, then pour the heated milk mixture over it, stirring to combine thoroughly. Allow the mixture to cool completely, then transfer covered to the refrigerator to chill thoroughly. Strain mixture through fine mesh strainer to remove solidified fat particles. Reserve in refrigerator.

SINGLE PORTION

WHITE CHOCOLATE MILK PUNCH

3¾oz (112.5ml) caramelized white chocolate milk

1oz (30ml) The Bitter Truth Apricot Liqueur

1oz (30ml) Christian Brothers Sacred Bond Brandy

¾oz (22.5ml) heavy cream

½oz (15ml) cinnamon bourbon

4 drops salt solution

Combine all ingredients with ice in cocktail shaker. Shake briefly until chilled and diluted, then double-strain into a medium serving glass.

BATCH

WHITE CHOCOLATE MILK PUNCH *(Serves 8)*

720g caramelized white chocolate milk

174g The Bitter Truth Apricot Liqueur

153g Christian Brothers Sacred Bond Brandy

126g heavy cream

72g cinnamon bourbon

2g salt solution

Combine all ingredients in medium bowl, stirring to mix thoroughly. Transfer to a glass bottle. Reserve in the refrigerator to chill thoroughly.

TO ASSEMBLE AND SERVE BATCH

Combine 5oz (150ml) of the chilled cocktail base with ice in cocktail shaker. Shake briefly until chilled and diluted, then double-strain into a medium serving glass.

GRASSHOPPER

WHITE CHOCOLATE SYRUP

200g water
100g white chocolate, coarsely chopped

Fill a large bowl with ice, and set a smaller bowl inside it. In a medium saucepan, combine the water and chocolate. Bring the mixture to a boil over medium-high heat, then pour the hot mixture into the bowl set in ice and allow it to cool completely. Cover the bowl with plastic wrap and transfer it to the refrigerator overnight. During this time, the fat in the chocolate will solidify and rise to the top of the mixture. The following day, strain the mixture through a mesh strainer, discarding the solidified chocolate fat. Transfer the mixture to a small bottle or an airtight container and reserve in the refrigerator.

←

We strain out the solidified chocolate fat here to avoid it contributing to a gritty, chunky texture in the final cocktail.

MINT VODKA

100g fresh mint
350g vodka, chilled thoroughly in the freezer before using

Fill a large pot with water and bring it to a boil. While the pot is heating, fill a large bowl with ice water. Pick the mint leaves from the stems, discarding the stems and any black or bruised leaves. Stir the leaves into the boiling water and boil them for 1 minute. After 1 minute, remove the leaves from the water with a strainer or slotted spoon and immediately transfer them to the bowl filled with ice water to halt their cooking. Once cooled, drain the leaves and transfer them to a paper towel. Cover them with a second paper towel, and squeeze gently to remove any excess water.

Transfer the blanched mint to a blender, and add the chilled vodka. Blend this mixture at high speed for 1 minute. (Blending at high speed has a tendency to heat liquids; we use pre-chilled vodka here to combat this, which helps keep the mint flavor bright and fresh.) Strain the mixture through a fine mesh strainer, discarding solids. Transfer to a glass bottle or an airtight container, and reserve it in the freezer to chill thoroughly.

←

This step – called *blanching* – kills enzymes in the mint to prevent them from browning. The process should not last more than a minute to avoid cooking the mint leaves, which would muddy their flavor.

GRASSHOPPER

1¼oz (37.5ml) mint vodka

1oz (30ml) Tempus Fugit Crème de Cacao

1oz (30ml) white chocolate syrup

¼oz (7.5ml) Ancho Reyes Verde Chile
   Poblano Liqueur

Combine all cocktail ingredients with ice in cocktail shaker. Shake until chilled and diluted, then double-strain into a medium serving glass.

GRASSHOPPER *(Serves 6)*

164g mint vodka

201g Tempus Fugit Crème de Cacao

194g white chocolate syrup

41g Ancho Reyes Verde Chile Poblano Liqueur

Combine all ingredients in a medium bowl, stirring to mix thoroughly. Transfer mixture to a glass bottle or other non-reactive airtight container. Reserve in the refrigerator.

TO ASSEMBLE AND SERVE BATCH

Combine 3½oz (105ml) of the cocktail base with ice in cocktail shaker. Shake until chilled and diluted, then double-strain into a medium serving glass.

FULTON CLUB PUNCH

PUNCH BASE BATCH
(Serves 8–10)

3 medium-sized navel oranges
240g sugar
1 large, ripe pineapple
1 bottle chardonnay
45g Pierre Ferrand 1840 Cognac
44g Rhine Hall Cherry Brandy
26g Pierre Ferrand Dry Curaçao
22g Smith & Cross Rum

Peel the oranges using a vegetable peeler, taking care to remove as little pith as possible. Reserve the peeled fruit for juicing. In a small bowl, combine the orange peels and sugar. Muddle this mixture with cocktail muddler or the end of a rolling pin. Allow to sit for 30 minutes, muddling and stirring periodically.

Meanwhile, peel the pineapple, remove the core, and chop into small chunks. Add the pineapple chunks to the orange peel mixture, muddling and mixing as before to thoroughly incorporate. Allow to sit for at least another 30 minutes (or up to overnight), muddling and stirring periodically.

In a large bowl, combine the remaining liquid ingredients, stirring to mix thoroughly. Pour this mixture over the pineapple mixture, stirring to dissolve sugar completely. Allow this to marinate for 10 minutes. Strain the mixture through a mesh strainer, pushing on solids to extract as much liquid as possible. Discard solids. Transfer to a glass bottle or other non-reactive airtight container and transfer to the refrigerator to chill thoroughly.

RASPBERRY CARDAMOM ICE BLOCK

5 whole cardamom pods
500g water
350g fresh raspberries
158g sugar
reserved peeled oranges

Place the cardamom pods onto a cutting board or countertop. Using a small saucepan, crush the pods lightly, then place them into the saucepan. Toast the cracked cardamom over medium heat until fragrant. Add the water, raspberries, and sugar and increase the heat to high. Bring the mixture to a boil. Boil for 6 minutes.

Meanwhile, fill a large bowl with ice, and set a smaller bowl inside it. Juice the oranges. Remove the raspberry mixture from the heat and add the orange juice, stirring to combine. Strain the mixture through a fine mesh strainer into the bowl set over ice, discarding solids. Allow the mixture to chill completely, then transfer it to a cake pan, baking dish, large mixing bowl, or other large vessel that will fit in your freezer. Freeze until completely solid. Reserve.

←

Depending on the acidity of the raspberries, you may want to include a squeeze of fresh lemon juice to this ice stock before freezing. Taste the mixture and adjust to your liking, keeping in mind that as the ice melts, it will influence the balance of the punch.

TO ASSEMBLE AND SERVE

two 750 ml bottles of sparkling white wine

Place the block of raspberry cardamom ice into a punch bowl or other large serving vessel. Pour the punch base down the side of the bowl. Gently add the bottles of sparkling wine, taking care to pour slowly so as not to encourage too much bubbling. Gently stir the mixture to incorporate thoroughly. Ladle the mixture into individual glasses and serve immediately.

Note: Much of the appeal of this punch is the refreshing carbonation it offers, which will dissipate if the punch is allowed to sit unconsumed for a long period of time. To prevent this, an alternative serving option is to refrain from adding the sparkling wine all at once, instead chilling it in a nearby bucket of ice and topping individual portions with it à la minute. A ratio of 1 part base to 2 parts sparkling wine per glass is ideal.

PARSNIP FLIP

**ALMOND
ANGOSTURA**

40g Angostura Aromatic Bitters

2g almond extract

In a small bowl, stir together Angostura and almond extract. Transfer to a small glass bottle or other non-reactive airtight container and reserve.

**TOASTED
ALMONDS**

70g slivered almonds

2g kosher salt

4g almond oil

Preheat oven to 400°F (205°C). Combine almond slivers, salt, and oil in medium bowl, tossing nuts to coat evenly. Spread almonds on sheet tray and toast in oven for about 12 minutes, or until deep brown and fragrant. Allow to cool completely.

← Canola oil can be substituted for almond oil if need be.

**ROASTED
PARSNIPS**

675g parsnips

137g butter, at room temperature

90g maple syrup

71g dark brown sugar

5g kosher salt

Preheat oven to 400°F (205°C). Scrub the parsnips to remove any dirt, and trim off the tops and bottom tips of each. Slice the parsnips into disks about ½ in (1.25 cm) thick.

Combine the softened butter, maple syrup, brown sugar, and salt in the bowl of a stand mixer. Using the paddle attachment, whip the mixture at medium speed until it's well-incorporated and fluffy. Stop the mixer and add the parsnip disks to the bowl, tossing to coat them thoroughly.

← If you don't have a stand mixer, a whisk and some good old-fashioned elbow grease will work here.

Line a sheet tray with parchment, and spread the parsnip disks onto it. Roast the parsnips in the oven for 40 minutes, stirring halfway through to ensure they cook evenly. Allow to cool completely.

**PARSNIP-
ALMOND SYRUP**

600g water

105g maple syrup

90g dark brown sugar

75g orange marmalade

In a medium saucepan, combine all ingredients along with the roasted parsnips (including any liquid from the roasting pan) and toasted almonds. Bring the mixture to a boil over medium heat, and boil for 3 minutes. Transfer the mixture to a food processor or a blender and pulse it a few times to break up the parsnips and almonds. Strain this mixture into a clean bowl, discarding solids. Transfer the liquid to a glass bottle or other non-reactive airtight container and transfer it to the refrigerator to chill it thoroughly.

← Contents may settle over time; this is normal. Give the mixture a good shake before using it.

PARSNIP FLIP

2oz (60ml) parsnip-almond syrup

1oz (30ml) Knob Creek Single Barrel Reserve
120 Proof Bourbon

¾oz (22.5ml) Lustau Pedro Ximénez San Emilio Sherry

2 dashes Angostura Aromatic Bitters

1 whole egg

Combine all ingredients in a cocktail shaker. Dry shake until frothy. Add ice and shake again vigorously until chilled and diluted, then double-strain into a medium serving glass. Add 5 drops of almond Angostura in a circle on the surface of the cocktail. Drag a tasting straw or toothpick through the drops to create a swirled pattern.

PARSNIP FLIP *(Serves 6)*

402g parsnip-almond syrup

150g Knob Creek Single Barrel Reserve
120 Proof Bourbon

150g Lustau Pedro Ximénez San Emilio Sherry

24g Angostura Aromatic Bitters

Combine all ingredients in medium bowl, stirring to mix thoroughly. Strain into glass bottle. Reserve at room temperature.

TO ASSEMBLE AND SERVE BATCH

Gather a medium serving glass. Combine 3¾oz (112.5ml) of the cocktail base and one whole egg in a cocktail shaker. Dry shake until frothy. Add ice and shake again vigorously until chilled and diluted, then double-strain into a medium serving glass. Add 5 drops of almond Angostura in a circle on the surface of the cocktail. Drag a tasting straw or toothpick through the drops to create a swirled pattern.

POLAR PLUNGE

CHOCOLATE VERMOUTH

100g Mancino Chinato Vermouth
10g unsweetened cocoa powder

Combine the vermouth and cocoa powder in a blender. Blend mixture on high speed for 1 minute, or until thoroughly incorporated. Strain the mixture through a fine mesh strainer, discarding any solids. Transfer the mixture to a small bottle or an airtight container and reserve in the refrigerator.

←

This mixture may settle out over time (which is normal); shake quickly before use to re-incorporate the cocoa powder.

POLAR PLUNGE
Single Portion

1½oz (45ml) Flor de Caña 12-year Aged Rum
¾oz (22.5ml) Tempus Fugit Crème de Cacao
¼oz (7.5ml) chocolate vermouth
¼oz (7.5ml) Fernet Branca Menta

Combine all ingredients with ice in a cocktail mixing glass. Stir until chilled and diluted, then strain into a medium serving glass.

POLAR PLUNGE
Batch (Serves 6)

255g Flor de Caña 12-year Aged Rum
144g Tempus Fugit Crème de Cacao
42g chocolate vermouth
42g Fernet Branca Menta
192g water

Combine all ingredients in a medium bowl, stirring to mix thoroughly. Transfer mixture to a glass bottle or other non-reactive airtight container. Reserve in the freezer to chill thoroughly.

To serve, pour approximately 4oz (120ml) of the chilled cocktail batch into a medium serving glass.

LATTE SPICED PUMPKIN

LATTE SPICED PUMPKIN BASE

55 g George Dickel Rye Whiskey

45 g Averna Amaro

70 g St. George NOLA Coffee Liqueur

Combine all ingredients in a small bowl, stirring to mix thoroughly. Cover and set aside.

LATTE SPICED PUMPKIN BATCH
(Serves 6)

4 eggs

40 g sugar

40 g light brown sugar

4 g salt

80 g canned pumpkin purée

215 g whole milk

Combine eggs, sugar, brown sugar, and salt in a medium bowl, whisking to mix thoroughly. Set aside.

Combine pumpkin purée and milk in a medium saucepan. Bring the mixture to a simmer over medium-high heat, taking care not to boil it outright (which could impart undesirable flavors from the scalded milk). Remove the saucepan from the heat.

Working in small increments at a time, slowly whisk the heated milk into the egg mixture.

Fill a small pot with an inch or so of water, and bring it to a simmer over medium-high heat. Place the bowl containing the pumpkin mixture over the simmering water and begin whisking (which helps prevent the eggs from curdling). Heat the mixture to around 155°F (70°C), or until it's uncomfortable to dip your finger into the mixture for more than a second or so, whisking constantly as it warms.

Remove from heat and transfer the mixture to a blender. Turn the blender on medium speed and add the cocktail base to incorporate it thoroughly.

At this point, the cocktail is ready and best served right away. If you need to hold it for a while, transfer it to a pre-warmed slow cooker set on low heat, or into a bowl set over simmering water. Be sure to whisk it or blend it with an immersion blender briefly to aerate it before portioning.

←

Take your time here; the reason we do this slowly is so we don't cook the eggs by suddenly introducing hot milk into them, which would end up yielding a bowl of scrambled eggs.

TO PORTION AND SERVE

instant espresso powder

Using a ladle, dole out servings into individual glasses. Garnish each with a pinch of instant espresso powder.

NACHO SHANDY

CILANTRO TEQUILA

200g Tequila Cabeza Blanco
20g cilantro stems

Combine tequila and cilantro stems in a mason jar or other non-reactive airtight container. Allow to infuse overnight. Strain mixture through a mesh strainer, discarding stems. Reserve.

CHILI CORN CHIP SPICE MIX

4g cumin seeds
15g Tostitos Hint Of Lime tortilla chips
20g kosher salt

In a medium saucepan, toast the cumin seeds over medium heat until fragrant. Transfer the toasted seeds to a spice grinder and grind to a fine powder. Transfer the powder to a small bowl and set aside.

Place the corn chips into the spice grinder and grind to a fine powder as well.

In a small bowl, combine the salt, corn chip powder, and 2g of the toasted cumin powder, stirring to combine. Transfer to a small airtight container and reserve.

HOT SAUCE ICE

360g water
90g Frank's RedHot cayenne pepper sauce
60g Ancho Reyes Ancho Chile Liqueur
60g fresh lime juice
30g sugar

Combine all ingredients in a medium bowl, whisking to mix thoroughly. Fill a 1¼ inch (3.2 cm) square ice mold with mixture. Freeze into cubes until completely solid. Reserve.

NACHO SHANDY

1 lime wedge

¾oz (22.5ml) cilantro tequila

¾oz (22.5ml) Pierre Ferrand Dry Curaçao

¾oz (22.5ml) fresh lime juice

½oz (15ml) agave syrup

¼oz (7.5ml) Cruz De Fuego Mezcal

4oz (120ml) Miller High Life, very cold

Wipe the outside rim of a serving glass with a lime wedge. Holding the glass with the rim facing slightly downwards, sprinkle the corn chip spice mix onto the outer rim of the glass. Place 3 hot sauce ice cubes into the glass.

Combine all ingredients (except beer) with ice in a cocktail shaker. Shake vigorously until chilled and diluted, then strain through a fine mesh strainer into the serving glass. Gently add the beer.

NACHO SHANDY BASE *(Serves 8)*

172g cilantro tequila

184g Pierre Ferrand Dry Curaçao

184g fresh lime juice

176g agave syrup

54g Cruz De Fuego Mezcal

120g water

Combine all ingredients in a medium bowl, stirring to mix thoroughly. Transfer to a glass bottle or other non-reactive airtight container, and transfer to the refrigerator to chill thoroughly.

TO ASSEMBLE AND SERVE BATCH

reserved cocktail base

36oz (3 bottles) Miller High Life, very cold

Combine the cocktail base and beer in a large pitcher.

Wipe the outside rim of a serving glass with a lime. Holding the glass with the rim facing slightly downwards, sprinkle the corn chip spice mix onto the outer rim of the glass. Place 3 hot sauce ice cubes into the glass. Pour the cocktail mixture from the pitcher into the glass. Repeat for remaining cocktail portions.

SALT
RIM

A tidy way to apply a salt or spice mix to the rim of a glass is to first remove a wedge from a whole lime. Position the lime so that the "lip" formed by the removed wedge only touches the outside of the rim. Rotate the glass to moisten the rim of it with the lime. Then, holding the glass with the rim facing downwards, sprinkle the spice mix onto the glass, rotating it as you sprinkle to cover the rim. This method ensures the mix is applied only onto the outside rim of the glass, which is visually-appealing and also prevents the spice mix from falling down into the beverage (which can cause an unpleasant, gritty texture).

KEY LIME PIE MIMOSA

CONDENSED MILK STOCK

100 g sweetened condensed milk

100 g warm water

2 g salt

Combine all ingredients in a small bowl, whisking to mix thoroughly. Reserve in the refrigerator.

TO ASSEMBLE AND SERVE

3 oz (90 ml) Prosecco

¾ oz (22.5 ml) Licor 43 Original

¾ oz (22.5 ml) fresh lime juice

1 oz (15 ml) condensed milk stock

1 graham cracker

Gently pour Prosecco into a tall champagne flute.

Combine vanilla liqueur, lime juice, and condensed milk stock with ice in cocktail shaker. Shake briefly until chilled and diluted, then strain into flute (do this final step gently and slowly, to avoid causing the Prosecco to bubble over). Garnish with a grating of graham cracker.

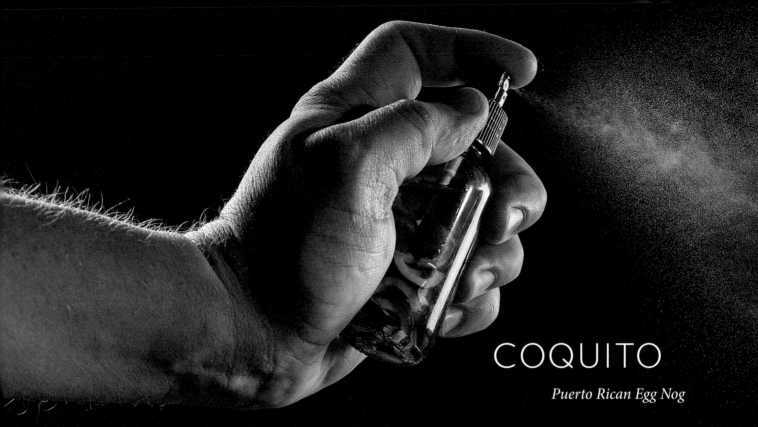

COQUITO

Puerto Rican Egg Nog

TOASTED COCONUT

100 g sweetened coconut flakes

Preheat an oven to 350°F (150°C). Spread the coconut flakes onto a cookie sheet or sheet tray. Toast the flakes in the oven, stirring occasionally, for about 15 minutes, or until brown and very fragrant. Let cool completely. Reserve.

COCONUT SPRAY

1 vanilla bean
35 g toasted coconut
100 g Sailor Jerry Spiced Rum

Cut the vanilla bean in half lengthwise with a sharp, small knife. Use the rear edge of the knife to scrape the tiny seeds from each pod half.

If you don't have sous vide equipment:
Combine the vanilla seeds and pods with the rum and coconut flakes in a non-reactive airtight container (a mason jar works well for this). Allow this mixture to steep for at least 4 days, shaking or stirring daily. After this time, place the jar in the freezer for 2 hours to solidify any coconut fat. Strain the mixture through a coffee filter, discarding solids. Transfer the strained liquid to a small glass spray bottle and reserve.

If you have an immersion circulator or sous vide bath:
Combine the vanilla seeds and pods with the rum and coconut flakes in a vacuum bag and seal. Cook en sous vide at 70°C (160°F) for at least 30 minutes. Meanwhile, prepare an ice bath. Transfer the bag to the ice bath to chill completely, then place the bag upright in the freezer for 2 hours, or until the coconut's fat solidifies. Using sharp scissors, cut a small incision in the bottom corner of the bag and drain the liquid contents through a coffee filter, leaving the solids behind. Transfer the strained liquid to a small glass spray bottle and reserve.

SPICED RUM

8g cinnamon sticks

1 whole star anise

2 whole allspice berries

5 whole cloves

1 vanilla bean

200g Sailor Jerry Spiced Rum

20g toasted coconut

In a medium saucepan, toast the cinnamon, star anise, allspice, and cloves over medium heat until fragrant. Let cool completely.

Cut the vanilla bean in half lengthwise with a sharp, small knife. Use the rear edge of the knife to scrape the tiny seeds from each pod half.

If you don't have sous vide equipment:
Combine all of the above ingredients with the rum and the toasted coconut in a non-reactive airtight container (a mason jar works well for this). Allow this mixture to steep for 4-7 days, shaking or stirring daily. After this time, strain the mixture through a fine mesh strainer, then through a coffee filter, discarding solids. Transfer the strained liquid to a glass bottle or other non-reactive airtight container and reserve.

If you have an immersion circulator or sous vide bath:
Combine all of the above ingredients with the rum and the toasted coconut in a vacuum bag and seal. Cook en sous vide at 80°C (175°F) for 1 hour. Meanwhile, prepare an ice bath. Transfer the bag to the ice bath to chill completely. Strain the mixture through a fine mesh strainer, discarding solids. Transfer the strained liquid to a glass bottle or other non-reactive airtight container and reserve.

COQUITO BATCH
(Serves 12)

392g (one 13.5oz can) coconut milk

375g (one 12oz can) evaporated milk

372g (one 14oz can) sweetened condensed milk

60g egg yolks

3g kosher salt

157g spiced rum

34g Clément Mahina Coco

Combine all the ingredients except the rums in the pitcher of a blender, and blend at high speed until thoroughly incorporated. With the blender running at low speed, slowly add the rums in small increments. Strain the mixture, and transfer to a glass bottle or other non-reactive airtight container. Reserve the mixture in the refrigerator to chill thoroughly before serving.

TO ASSEMBLE AND SERVE

Add 3.5oz (105ml) of the chilled cocktail base and one cube of ice to a cocktail shaker. Shake vigorously, then double-strain into a small serving glass. Garnish with a few sprays of coconut spray.

←

Mixing alcohol with dairy products often causes them to curdle suddenly. While there are some techniques for which this behavior is desirable (e.g. milk punches), we want to avoid it here. Adding the rums in small, slow increments helps incorporate them smoothly into the rest of this mixture.

HOT CHOCOLATE

+ Non-Alcoholic Recipe

ALCOHOLIC
↓

NON-ALCOHOLIC (N/A)
↓

HOT CHOCOLATE BASE BATCH *(Serves 6)*

76g Yellow Chartreuse

54g Green Chartreuse

17g Dumante Verdenoce Pistachio Liqueur

16g golden raisins

12g Tempus Fugit Crème de Cacao

10g fresh ginger, peeled and sliced thinly

6g The Bitter End Mexican Mole Bitters

Combine all ingredients in a medium saucepan and bring to a simmer over medium heat. Remove from heat, cover, and allow the mixture to cool for 1 hour. Strain through a mesh strainer, discarding solids. Transfer to a glass bottle or other non-reactive airtight container and reserve.

→

While we prefer the nuanced sweetness offered by Dumante Pistachio Liqueur for this recipe, an amaretto (almond) liqueur can be used as a reasonable substitute if need be.

N/A HOT CHOCOLATE BASE BATCH *(Serves 6)*

250g water

125g golden raisins

150g fresh ginger, peeled and sliced thinly against the fibers

65g sugar

Combine all ingredients in a medium saucepan, and bring to a simmer over medium heat. Remove from heat, cover, and allow the mixture to cool for 1 hour. Strain through a mesh strainer, discarding solids. Transfer to a glass bottle or other non-reactive airtight container and reserve.

WHITE CHOCOLATE
WHIPPED CREAM

150 g whole milk

100 g white chocolate, coarsely chopped

15 g sugar

2 g kosher salt

190 g heavy cream *(estimated)*

Fill a large bowl with ice, and set a smaller bowl inside it. In a medium saucepan, combine all of the ingredients except the cream. Bring the mixture to a boil over medium-high heat, stirring constantly to prevent the milk from scorching. Pour the hot mixture into the bowl set in ice and allow it to cool completely. Cover the bowl with plastic wrap and transfer it to the refrigerator overnight. During this time, the fat in the chocolate will solidify and rise to the top of the mixture.

When ready to assemble this cocktail, strain the mixture through a mesh strainer, discarding the solidified chocolate fat. Add equal weight cream (about 190 g) and stir to combine. Transfer the mixture to the bowl of a stand mixer. Using the whisk attachment, whip the mixture at high speed until the mixture thickens and becomes aerated (it should be thick but still pourable). Reserve chilled until ready to serve.

←

This step can also be done in a cocktail shaker. Remove the spring from a Hawthorne strainer and place it in the shaker tin with the white chocolate mixture. Shake until mixture thickens but is still pourable. This will take some time, but the spring, acting as a whisk, helps speed up the process.

CHOCOLATE
MILK

368 g whole milk

60 g roasted pistachio kernels

33 g sugar

2 g kosher salt

60 g dark chocolate, chopped into small pieces

Combine all ingredients (except the chocolate) in a medium saucepan. Bring the mixture to a boil over medium heat, stirring constantly to avoid scorching the milk. Once the mixture reaches a boil, remove it from the heat and add the chocolate, stirring until it's completely melted. Transfer the mixture to a blender, and blend on high speed for 1 minute, or until the mixture is completely smooth.

At this point, the mixture should still be warm and is ready to be portioned and served. If you need to hold it for a while before serving, allow it to cool to room temperature, then store it in the refrigerator. You'll need to re-warm it gently in a saucepan before proceeding to the final assembly of the cocktail, stirring constantly to prevent burning.

TO PORTION
AND SERVE
BATCH

Preheat an oven to 170°F (75°C). Gather 6 coffee mugs or tea cups, and warm them in the oven for at least 15 minutes.

In a blender or a large bowl, combine the chocolate milk mixture and the cocktail base, blending or whisking to incorporate thoroughly. Transfer 4½ oz (135 ml) of the cocktail mixture to a warmed mug, and top with a large spoonful of white chocolate whipped cream. Repeat for remaining mugs.

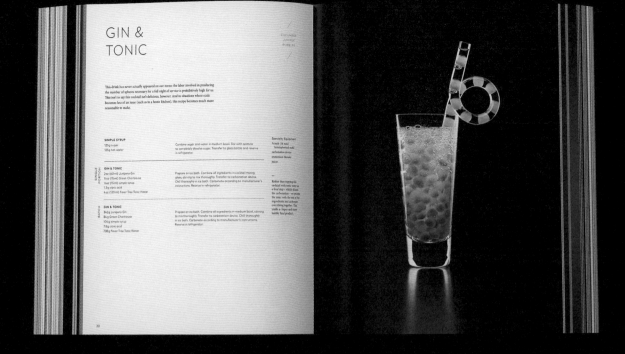

The world's most innovative cookbook *is about* COCKTAILS

Over
440 beautiful pages

Featuring more than
100 delicious, innovative recipes

COLOPHON

This first edition, first printing of
The Aviary: Holiday Cocktails
was printed by Shenzhen Artron Color Printing Co. Ltd. of Shenzhen, China.

Prepress by iocolor, LLC of Seattle, Washington.

Recipe creation and testing:
MICAH MELTON and **INGI SIGURDSSON**

Project management:
ALEX HAYES and **JOSH HARTLEY**

Written by:
ALLEN HEMBERGER and **NICK KOKONAS**

Design and photography:
SARAH and **ALLEN HEMBERGER**
Small Batch Creative, LLC | www.smallbatchcreative.com | art@smallbatchcreative.com

Published by:
The Alinea Group, LLC | www.thealineagroup.com

Printed using stochastic color separation and Chroma Centric inks on 120 gsm Dadong Woodfree FSC paper. Typefaces used include FF Mark, Filosofia, Minion Pro, and Verlag.

ISBN-13: 978-1-7330088-0-8